JOHN CONSTABLE

ABOUT THE AUTHOR

Phoebe Pool took her degree in the History of Art at the
Courtauld Institute of Art in London. She has written a book
'Picasso: the formative years' in collaboration with Sir Anthony
Blunt and is now at work on a study of Dégas and his
early literary and artistic background.

PHOEBE POOL

John Constable

BARNES & NOBLE

B&N

1873

ART SERIES

BARNES & NOBLE, INC.

NEW YORK

Publishers • Booksellers • Since 1873

Editor: Anthony Bosman
Lay-out: Wim van Stek and Aart Verhoeven
Published in the United States in 1964
by Barnes & Noble, Inc., 105 Fifth Avenue, New York 3, N.Y.
© 1963 and printed in Holland by The Ysel Press Ltd, Deventer

JOHN CONSTABLE

There may have been greater British artists than John Constable, but, as Roger Fry points out, he is the only Englishman who has added something considerable to the idiom of European painting. Artists and writers do sometimes find nourishment for their work (and see imaginary splendours) in feeble and eccentric products by their contemporaries. Nevertheless it is scarcely a sign of dullness or mediocrity in Constable that he won praise from Stendhal, Géricault, Blake and Coleridge, and caused the fiery Delacroix to repaint part of his Salon picture "The Massacre of Scio" and to write in his journal: "This man Constable has done me a power of good." *("Ce Constable me faisait un grand bien".)*

Apart from Constable's historical and European significance, to which we must return, what is the *grand bien,* or especial pleasure, to be derived from his work? It lies, perhaps, in a heightened, more intense and exact perception or remembrance of *particular* English places, seasons, tricks of light and weather. "No two days are alike," he wrote, "not even two hours; neither were there ever two leaves of a tree alike since the creation of the world." This sharpened feeling for the local and particular links Constable with other great figures in the heroic period of early Romanticism, with his contemporary, Wordsworth, who described the power within him as "a local spirit of his own, at war with general tendency", or with William Blake, scribbling furiously on Reynolds' *Discourses :* "All knowledge is particular . . . Generalising in everything the man would soon be a fool." Constable quickly perceived the gulf between what he was attempting to do and the aims of the other great Suffolk painter, Thomas Gainsborough ("With particulars he had nothing to do; his object was to deliver a fine sentence"), although in fact he greatly loved Gainsborough's art, was much influenced by it (p. 20) and in his youth fancied that he "found Gainsborough in every hedge and hollow tree".

When Constable wrote in his well-known letter of 1802, "I shall endeavour to get a pure and unaffected manner of representing the scenes that may employ me . . . there is room enough for a natural painter. The great vice of the present day is bravura, an attempt to do something beyond the truth", the battle was only just beginning; ideas of the lofty, idealized subject died hard. In 1820 Henry Fuseli, lecturing at the Royal Academy, could still speak of "the last branch of uninteresting subjects, that kind of landscape which is entirely occupied with the tame delineation of a given spot", and even after Constable's death, Ruskin, angry that C. R. Leslie (Constable's biographer) had rated him above his beloved Turner, would only admit that Constable had a sort of sincerity and "might be able to give a cheap, deceptive resemblance of nature as seen through the eyes of a faun or a hart". This was most unjust, for Constable's local affections and realistic factual details were almost always unified and subordinated to the general architecture of the picture and to the effect which he wished to produce. He derived this power, as we shall see, from his study of the great traditional landscape painters, not least Claude Lorrain, whose "Hagar and the Angel" shown to him by Sir George Beaumont about 1795 he copied, and whose habit of framing the countryside between two groups of trees he frequently borrowed, as in "Valley of the Stour, with Dedham in the Distance" (p. 21).

It was peculiarly inept of Ruskin to compare Constable's vision with the perceptions of an animal since (here again, like that of his poetical contemporaries) his contemplation of the countryside was a solemn, quasi-religious experience which enabled him, like Coleridge,

> from outer forms to win
> The passion and the life whose fountains are within.

Particularly in later years, he was using nature to body forth the stormy dramas and exaltations of his own spirit:

> O lady, we receive but what we give,
> And in our life alone does nature live,
> Ours is her wedding garment, ours her shroud.

Constable himself compared his art with that of Coleridge. When David's supporter, Délécluze, wrote a notice complaining that Constable's pictures were like those rich preludes in music, "full harmonious warblings of the Aeolian lyre which mean nothing", the painter retorted in a letter to his friend John Fisher: "Is not some of this *blame* the highest *praise* — what is poetry? What is Coleridge's 'Ancient Mariner' *(the very best modern poem)* but something like this?"

Constable must certainly have known both Wordsworth and Coleridge, who, when staying with Fisher in 1821, irritated his host extremely by saying, "there were some parts of your [Constable's] last picture good". Wordsworth, Coleridge and Constable had all abandoned the eighteenth-century mechanistic view of the world, together with the well-worn mythologies of nymphs and goddesses. They were alone with the countryside, as the early Protestants had been with God, and felt the moral grandeur of nature, even in its sober and humble manifestations, so that when describing Constable's art, it has become almost obligatory to speak of Wordsworth's

> feeling and a love
> That had no need of a remoter charm
> By thought supplied, nor any interest
> Unborrowed from the eye.

Certainly Wordsworth and Constable must have met about 1806-7 through the latter's patron, Sir George Beaumont, but some writers (e.g., Mr. Morse Peckham) have tried to make the connection between them rather closer and more decisive than the facts warrant. I would only assert that one can scarcely hope to understand Constable's attitude to landscape without remembering the feelings he shared with the heroic generation of Romantic poets. These feelings, together with his respect for pictorial form and tradition, prevented his works from becoming a mere sum of factual observations and trivial details. "It is the business of a painter", he wrote, "not to contend with nature and put his scene (a valley filled with imagery fifty miles long) on a canvas of a few inches, but to make something out of nothing in attempting which he must almost of necessity become poetical."

Constable was born at East Bergholt, Suffolk, in 1776, the second son of a prosperous miller. His birthplace is shown on page 40. He went to school in the beautiful village of Lavenham, where, owing to the negligence of a lovesick headmaster, the boys were cruelly flogged. This may have had some permanent effect on the artist by creating a feeling of rebellion against authority in a nature that was, in other respects, full of traditional piety and conservatism. (In 1832 Constable, like many contemporaries, was horrified at the prospect of the Reform Bill.) Years later, asked by an engraver if he might make a plate from his portrait of a different headmaster, Constable burst out, "Who would ever pay for the portrait of a turnkey at Newgate who had ever been in such a place?" After Lavenham, until about 1793, he went to the Grammar School at Dedham; here his achievement was mediocre, but he found indulgence for his growing love of painting. At this time he became friendly with a plumber and glazier called John Dunthorne and painted from nature in his company.

He was also encouraged by Sir George Beaumont, whose mother lived at Dedham. Sir George not only owned the Claude Lorrain mentioned above, but had made a small collection of drawings by Thomas Girtin, which he advised Constable to study "as examples of great breadth and truth". Girtin was only one year older than Constable, but he had developed more quickly and was beginning to revolutionize landscape painting in water colour, taking it far away from the tinted drawings of the eighteenth century. He had a great instinct for the total unity and design of a picture, for simplicity and for wide sweeps of empty foreground. In later life Constable praised him in his lectures, and, as early as 1801, in the Derbyshire sketches showed that he had begun to learn from him. Girtin's spaciousness and narrow range of tones —dark greens, browns and purples—are perhaps even more noticeable in Constable's drawings of the Lake District executed in 1806 (p. 22) and in the simple massing of tones which characterizes "Malvern Hall" of 1809. Incidentally, Constable, like Cézanne, could not paint at his best when away from his familiar surroundings and he told Leslie that the solitude of the mountains oppressed him. He was, in general, most stirred by a countryside with human activity (as p. 34, the drawing which shows the entrance to Salisbury). Auden's "friendless and unbrothered stone" attracted him less than the rich human

SELF-PORTRAIT
1806; pencil; $7\frac{1}{4} \times 5\frac{1}{2}$ in.; collection of Col. J. H. Constable

associations of the Stour country—"These scenes made me a painter and I am grateful", he wrote. At the time of his introduction to Beaumont (and through him to Lorrain and Girtin) Constable was working in his father's mill where he won a reputation for strength and was known by the local girls as "the handsome miller".

In 1795 Constable (probably aided by Beaumont) persuaded his father to let him try his chances in London, and there he met and was encouraged by J. T. (Antiquity) Smith, an engraver and typographical draughtsman. During the next three years, which were divided between London and his work as a miller, he kept in touch with Smith's advice and his letters show that even in Suffolk he was studying anatomy, drawing from plaster casts and reading books such as *Leonardo da Vinci* and Gessner's *Essay on Landscape*. A sketchbook of eleven pen drawings dated 1796, now in the Victoria and Albert Museum, shows that he then shared Smith's delight in picturesque "neglected fast-ruinating cottages" with their rough textures and flickering light effects. Smith had sometimes visited Gainsborough and owned a number of Gainsborough's drawings. His own book *Remarks on Rural Scenery with Twenty Etchings of Cottages from Nature* advocated the "matching" of outdoor colours, especially green, and made at least one observation from which Constable may have profited, an idea later more fully developed by the French Impressionists: "The colour of every object in nature is to be painted as partaking more or less of the colour of the objects to which it stands exposed."

It was not until February, 1799, that Constable finally gave up his work as a miller and returned to London with a letter of introduction to Joseph Farington, a pupil and follower of Richard Wilson. Constable conceived an immense admiration for Wilson, whom he described as "one of the great, who show to the world what exists in nature but was not known until his time", and in 1823 rather oddly declared: "He is now walking arm in arm with Milton and Linnaeus." (One wonders whether Wilson would, in fact, have enjoyed this strange promenade.) Farington lent Constable "Hadrian's Villa", which he copied, together with two other Wilsons. Some of his early landscapes (about 1802) recall Wilson in their use of fat pigment and warm yellow light. Farington also helped Constable by giving him a letter of recommendation to Wilton, keeper of the Royal Academy, and he wrote to Dunthorne, pleased at his admission: "The figure which I drew for admittance was the Torso . . . I shall begin painting as soon as I have the loan of a sweet little picture by Jacob Ruysdael to copy."

At this time Constable's work was rather backward for a student of twenty-two; in three years, Turner, who was only twenty-three, would be elected to the Royal Academy, and in 1800 John Sell Cotman was already beginning to exhibit at the Academy. But the time spent in the Suffolk mills had not been a dead loss, for it probably contributed to Constable's highly accurate rendering of transitory weather effects, and it was there that he thought of scenes to paint, for which his training at the Academy would later provide the technical means. He wrote to Dunthorne: "I find it necessary to fag at copying some time yet to acquire execution. The more facility of practice I get the more pleasure I shall find in my art; without the power of execution I should be continually embarrassed and it would be a burthen to me." He was right, for as yet his tentative and clumsy technique by no means equalled the fresh natural vision which can be glimpsed in such works as the Dedham Vale of 1802 (p. 21). This was the time of which he wrote in 1802 that he had been "running after nature at second hand". Apart from Claude, Wilson, Girtin and Gainsborough (whose early "Dutch" manner is echoed in "A Woody Road" (1800) and "The Edge of a Wood" (1802) (Toronto), particularly in the individual delineation of leaves), the painters through whose works Constable saw nature "at second hand" included Ruysdael, Cozens ("He is all poetry", said Constable), the Caracci and Van der Velde, of whom there are reminiscences in his works done on a sea-trip between London and Deal in 1803. In Suffolk it is easy to feel a natural affinity and contact with Holland, nursed as this was by centuries of sea trade, and Andrew Shirley well says that, before Constable, Gainsborough had found in Dutch painting "a cousin's approach to woodland and heath scenery under cool grey skies". This was the Gainsborough Constable approved, not, as he said, "the later Gainsborough, so wide of nature", and he followed him in his love of the Dutch, particularly of the sombre and spacious landscapes of Ruysdael.

As we have already seen, Constable developed slowly, and though occasionally a happy treatment of some congenial subject such as "Shipping in the Orwell" (c. 1806, p. 24) seems to foreshadow his later skill and felicity, on the whole he only began to attain his full stature after 1811. The many early portraits painted for money are often inept and poorly modelled; like a child drawing, Constable seems to find it difficult to attach his sitters' heads to their shoulders, though he could sometimes do better, as can be seen in the picture of his future wife, Maria Bicknell (p. 39), and it has often been said that the altar-pieces for Brantham Church, in the current historical style, are akin to that of Benjamin West (1804) and are barely worth visiting. As already mentioned, the sketches of the Lake District (1806) owed much to Girtin, whose example helped Constable to attain that broader, less detailed rendering of form which is to be seen in "View in Borrowdale" (p. 22). Many of his paintings in the next three years depended on these sketches, which are generally considered to show a great advance on the tentative, if more delicate, drawings done in Derbyshire in 1801.

It was a further gain for his technique that in 1807 Constable was asked to copy the family portraits of Lord Dysart, including several by Joshua Reynolds, whom we know he greatly admired (see p. 46). This seems to have led him to a bolder, looser, more fluid handling of paint, to a greater range of colours and to an increasing freedom, which was to be maintained until about 1826. But already his interest in passing atmospheric effects had been aroused, and he had begun the practice of recording the effect of sky and time of day which are generally and rightly associated with the Hampstead tree and sky studies of 1821-22. Thus on the back of the "View in Borrowdale" (p. 22) he wrote: "tone very mellow like the mildest of Gaspar Poussin and Sir G(eorge) B(eaumont) and on the whole deeper toned than this drawing," and on another: "Dark autumnal day at noon—tone more blooming than this—the effect exceeding terrific." This self-correction when he felt he had not truthfully represented what was there, this careful hoarding of the actual, is somehow a very nineteenth-century trait and reminds one of Degas' early colour notes on landscape, and even, to some extent, of the more intense particularism found in Gerard Manley Hopkins' notebooks. All these men were, in their different ways, more interested in truth than in the agreeable. In Constable's case it has often been pointed out that only at a moment of balance between science and faith could such complete confidence in nature exist. In later years he was to write: "In such an age as this, painting should be understood, not looked on with blind wonder, nor considered only as a poetic aspiration, but as a pursuit, legitimate, scientific and mechanical . . . . Imagination alone never did, and never can, produce works that are to stand by a comparison with realities". With one foot still in the optimistic eighteenth century, Constable could still write of nature as reflecting the mind of "the Divine Architect", and the blossoming of spring turned his thoughts to Christ. "Everything seems full of blossom of some kind, and at every step I take, and on whatever object I turn my eyes, that sublime expression of the Scriptures 'I am the resurrection and the life' seems as if uttered near me."

The period of Constable's development, which had opened with the upright Dedham Vale of 1802 and with his avowed project of being "a natural painter", culminates in the large, oblong "Dedham Vale" of 1811 (p. 23). Constable is no longer running after nature at second hand, but when he painted broad meadows with the sun falling across them, as he often did in the summer of 1812, one can still feel behind them the example of Rubens, particularly, perhaps, of the "Château de Steen", owned by Sir George Beaumont, which was one of Constable's favourite pictures. Even more remarkable in their rich atmospheric quality, vigour of handling and unity achieved by lighting are the oil sketches such as the stormy "Flatford Mill from a Lock on the Stour" (p. 25). Constable did not invent the oil sketch, which had been used by both his admired Rubens and Gainsborough, but he exploited its possibilities as a means of exploring nature and as a picture in its own right. He seems to have recognised, and to have hinted at, the fact that his oil sketches were different in kind from those of pre-

13

vious artists. Oil sketches were particularly suitable for preserving the fresh immediacy of his first impression; he felt strongly that "a good thing can never be done twice", and these studies all derive from a direct visual experience.

At this time his drawings were perhaps somewhat arid in comparison with the oil sketches, but two long summers spent at East Bergholt (1813 and 1814) resulted in the marvellous pocket sketchbooks, from one of which "View on the Stour" (p. 26) is taken. Sketching "picturesque" scenes had been fashionable in the eighteenth century, but those vignettes were done as ends in themselves, whereas Constable's pencil sketches and water colours were used in preparation for oil paintings; they convey a complex and fleeting atmosphere and helped him to choose the motive for a large picture. His power of minute observation seems akin to that of one of his favourite poets, William Cowper, and still more to the affectionate particularism of Gilbert White's *Natural History of Selborne*. Of this, Constable wrote: "The mind that produced the Selborne is such a one as I have always envied—one that takes his observations from the subject itself and not from the writings of others. The single page of the life of Mr. White leaves a more lasting impression on my mind than all that has been written of Charles V." The sketchbook of 1814 is less detailed and has more broad massing of light and shade; here are the germs for many much later pictures and here too he worked out the plan for "Boat-building near Flatford Mill" (p. 42). Neither in this work nor in the "Boys Fishing" has he quite managed to preserve in a big picture what he called "the chiaroscuro of nature" and in spite of the surer brushwork of "Boat-building", painted entirely in the open air, this still seems rather an accumulation of details than a unified whole, darker in tone and less sparkling than the oil sketches.

Constable had a somewhat pessimistic and anxious temperament but he often had something to worry about—the opposition of his fiancée's (Maria Bicknell) family to their marriage, his wife's ill health and early death and, throughout his career, his lack of success as a painter in comparison with several contemporary mediocrities. But one sometimes gets the impression that he had the habit of assuming the worst. In

1797 he was writing despairingly to Smith: "And now I see plainly it will be my lot to walk through life in a path contrary to that in which my inclination would lead me"; yet his prosperous and indulgent father agreed to his career as a painter less than two years later. But our impression of Constable is not always improved by the intervention of his biographer Leslie, determined to make him a martyr, and a martyr of ineffable mildness. When Constable's diction is not muffled by the rather sentimental conventions of the day (so that his family are invariably the "dear, dear children"), he does not sound mild at all, but pungent and direct, and like so many painters, endowed with a gift for words. The spire of Salisbury "at fifteen miles off darted up into the sky like a needle". David and his followers "exhibited their stock and heartless petrifaction of men and women." Some contemporary painting is "the pastoral of the opera house". Many found his conversation egoistical and argumentative, and one can perhaps see in the paintings that he was a slow, ruminant thinker rather than a man of swift and epigrammatic mind. As so often happens, in some of his best observations on other artists, he seems to be describing himself.

Constable showed considerable originality in his oil sketches at a time when his full-dress pictures for the Academy were still somewhat tame and derivative. At least three years before the highly finished "Boat-building" (p. 42), "Flatford Mill from a Lock on the Stour" (about 1811) (p. 25) has a space composition based directly on nature, constructed from converging orthogonals, and closed in at the end by the poplar trees. The intervals are more true to nature, less precise and stylized than in a Claude Lorrain or Rubens, although, as Michael Kitson points out, Constable may have taken the space composition from one of the Angerstein seaports by Claude, selecting, however, only what was needed for his purpose. In the past Constable had emulated Gainsborough's brushwork so that the surface was unified by reducing everything in the picture to a common character, but in "Flatford Mill from a Lock on the Stour" consistency of texture is secured with the addition of greater variety and particularisation in shapes, tones and colours.

15

The subject of this oil sketch was not new; it had been explored by Morland, Crome and other followers of the picturesque, but to Constable it was less piquant or novel than a scene which he had loved deeply long before he painted any pictures. "The sound of water escaping from mill-dams etc., willows, old rotten planks, slimy posts and brickwork, I love such things. As long as I do paint I shall never cease to paint such places . . . painting is with me but another word for feeling, and I associate 'my careless boyhood' with all that lies on the banks of the Stour; these scenes made me a painter and I am grateful."

Years before, in 1800, Constable had met Maria Bicknell, a young granddaughter of the Rector at East Bergholt. In 1811 they wished to get married, but her family were on bad terms with Golding Constable and, also, considered the painter's prospects too uncertain, an attitude which at first Maria shared. "Indeed my dear John", she wrote, "people cannot now live on four hundred a year—it is a bad subject and therefore adieu to it." At this time Constable was trying to better his fortunes by painting portraits, and his devoted mother so little understood his objective that she could write: "Fortune seems now to place the ball at your feet, and I trust you will not kick it from you. You now so greatly excel in portraits that I hope you will pursue a path the most likely to bring you fame and wealth, by which you can alone expect to obtain the object of your fondest wishes." But Constable, despite depression, spent the summer months in Suffolk, this year on even more profitable and concentrated sketching than usual. To Maria he wrote: "It is many years since I have worked with so much steadiness or confidence. I hope you will see me an artist some time or another." This was probably the period when he painted the fresh and evocative "Spring, East Bergholt Common" (p. 27) and "Shipping in the Orwell" (p. 24).

The death of his mother in 1815 and the illness of his father meant that Constable was forced to stay in Suffolk, and the separation from Maria put a new strain on him. On one of his short trips to London in the summer of 1816 he seems to have painted the portrait sketch of her which is now in the Tate Gallery (p. 39). Constable's useful friend and supporter Archdeacon Fisher seems to have persuaded him to go ahead, and in October, 1811, Fisher himself married them, after which they went to stay with him at his vicarage of Osmington near Weymouth. There are pencil sketches which seem to have been made on his honeymoon, e.g., "Osmington Bay" (p. 28) and another view of the same shoreline appears in the oil sketch "Weymouth Bay" (p. 29), now in the National Gallery. This work is perhaps open to Constable's own criticism: "If the sky is obtrusive as mine are it is bad; but if it is evaded as mine are not, it is worse; it must and always shall with me make an effectual part of the composition. It will be difficult to name a class of landscape in which the sky is not the key-note, the standard of scale, and the chief organ of sentiment."

Constable's marriage seems to have brought greater self-assurance into his work and the twelve years with Maria were probably both his happiest and his most mature and productive as a painter. At this time Rubens, whose work he had loved especially since seeing Beaumont's "Chateau de Stein" in 1804, seems to have been his chief model in maintaining a balance between the large masses and the details, and in the bright colours and boldness and breadth of design. In the "Flatford Mill", now in the National Gallery, the eye can travel through the picture as in a Rubens, though in this picture there is still, perhaps, somewhat too much particularized detail imperfectly fused into a whole.

A new phase of Constable's art opened in 1819, the year in which he became an associate of the Royal Academy (long after many of his more mediocre fellow painters) and exhibited "The White Horse", the first of a series of six-foot canvasses which was to include "The Hay Wain". Constable was enough a man of his own time to see the necessity for painting large full-scale works. "I do not consider myself at work", he wrote to Fisher, "unless I am before a six-foot canvas", and thereafter he tried to prepare for the Academy one at least of these monumental works every year. But at first it was difficult to carry the freshness and immediacy of the oil sketches into the larger, more finished, pictures, and others besides Kenneth Clark have considered "The White Horse" somewhat dry and diffuse. However, at the time it attracted more attention than had previous works by Constable, and an author in the *Literary Chronicle* wrote: "He does not give a sentiment, a soul to the exterior of nature, as Mr. Turner does ... he has none of the poetry of nature like Mr. Turner, but he has more of her portraiture." His next large work, "Stratford Mill", relies more on the dramatic contrast between the sombre mass of trees and the sparkling water and sky, but for Constable it is almost artificial in a somewhat Turneresque manner.

In "The Hay Wain" (1821) (p. 33) Constable at last managed to retain the fresh realism of the sketches in a large finished picture. He wrote of it to Fisher: "It has a more novel look than I expected." The picture probably originated in a sketch of Willy Lott's house painted about 1814, but in the new picture the empty meadows and the water have dwarfed the rôle of the house. For "The Hay Wain" Constable made an oil study about the size of the finished work (p. 32) with a greater boldness and freedom of touch and, in general, more nervous agitation and expressive power than was shown in the final work. But Kenneth Clark reminds us that many enduring qualities were added in the final version—the range of colour is greatly enlarged, the planes, particularly in the middle distance, are more firmly established, and the composition is made more classical and logical, the rhythms are larger and slower and an added stress on the horizontals confirms the feeling of pastoral midday calm. "The Hay Wain" was not sold, and its novelty did not strike the English critics as it later did the French.

Constable's financial position had improved after the death of his parents; also, his wife had an allowance from her grand-father and eventually inherited money from him. His state of relative financial security has often been contrasted with the hand-to-mouth existence of the Impressionists, in their early and exploratory phase. But on the debit side, it should be remembered that while the Impressionists benefited from an atmosphere of mutual criticism, and well understood what each other was about (though at one time Manet believed Renoir had no talent and that their friends should urge him to stop painting), few of Constable's friends really *did* understand what he was doing. Although they supported him, they did

18   (Continued on page 73)

19

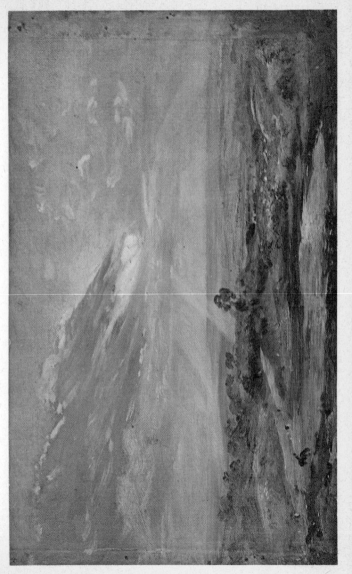

49

64

so rather blindly, and they seem to have shared the general impression that his pictures were unfinished, and that he just did not take the trouble to paint in the details. But as Sidney Key observes, this characteristic was intentional; Constable was painting the total visual impression of a landscape in terms of tone, not of accumulated detail, and the sharp definition of individual objects had to be subordinated to over-all effects, and to his novel, shorthand description of form. Even the loyal Fisher wrote of a landscape Constable had given him: "It does not solicit attention; and this I think true of all your pictures, and the real cause of your want of popularity." Though not all of them were able to appreciate him fully as an artist, Constable had staunch friends, particularly this same Archdeacon Fisher, his uncle the Bishop of Salisbury and Charles Leslie, his admiring biographer. Farington and Benjamin West also gave him good advice: the former recommended him to "unite firmness with freedom and avoid flimsiness" and "as he had been studying particular appearances, now to think of atmosphere and general effect", and West said: "Always remember, sir, that light and shadow *never stand still.*"

Beaumont's collection and his encouragement were important, but he must have been somewhat baffled by the mature Constable's art, and we are told that he asked Constable, "Do you not find it difficult to know where to place your brown tree?" By the period of which we are writing Constable had managed to escape the brown tree and the whole tradition which it represented.

Although Constable did not actually settle permanently in Hampstead until 1827, he was accustomed during the early twenties to move there in the summer with his somewhat delicate wife and young children, and Hampstead is perhaps particularly associated with his studies of clouds (see e.g. p. 37), many of them painted in 1821-22, which are among the more original of his achievements. As Kurt Badt has observed, before the Romantic movement painters had generally exploited the transient instability of clouds, changing them into decorative ribbons, waves or crests of foam; both Titian and Poussin produced majestic cloud structures, but in neither case were their skies naturalistically possible, and even Cozens "studies clouds in order to make an effect with them, not because he was interested in their true forms as such". The Romantics were naturally interested emotionally in the distant, the changing, the indefinite nature of clouds, which seemed to symbolise their own yearnings, but some of them, such as Constable and later Ruskin, were also interested in a different, more scientific way. Thus, Ruskin observes in Modern landscape "much attention to the real form of clouds and careful drawing of effects of mist; so that the appearance of objects as seen through it becomes a subject of science with us", and Constable in his lectures emphasised this side of art: "I hope to show that landscape painting is a regularly taught profession; that it is scientific as well as poetic"; and again: "In such an age as this, painting should be understood, not looked on with blind wonder, nor considered only as a poetic aspiration, but as a pursuit, legitimate, scientific and mechanical."

Constable's systematic studies of clouds are nearly all annotated on the back with such particular details as "Sept. 24th 10 o'clock morning wind S.W., warm and fine until afternoon when it rained and wind got more to the north". A letter of 1836 shows that he had read Thomas Forster's *Researches about Atmospheric Phenomena,* originally published in 1812, and Badt has suggested that he also read and was influenced by Luke Howard's *The Climate of London* (1818-20). His training as a miller must also have played a part. The mingling of scientific exactitude and poetic perception is well shown in a note which he wrote about his picture "Spring" mezzotinted by David Lucas, containing a sky rendered in more detail than that shown on page 27 and based on one of these cloud studies: "It may perhaps give some idea of one of those bright and silver days in spring, when at noon large garish clouds surcharged with hail or sleet sweep with their broad shadows the fields, woods and hills; and by their depth enhance the value of the vivid greens and yellows so peculiar to the season." Constable then goes on to describe the "natural history" of the hail squalls of that time of year. Constable's skies, unlike those of Poussin, Titian or Rubens, are only compatible with the particular atmosphere and weather to which he has joined them, and their realism reminds one that Constable's younger brother said, "When I look at a mill painted by John, I see that it will *go round*".

Of the large Academy pictures which Constable had resolved to do each year, "Waterloo Bridge" gave him the most trouble. He painted many versions of it (pp. 54, 55) and deliberated over it for some fifteen years, before it was finally exhibited in the Royal Academy Exhibition of 1832. The majestic sweep of sky is here very impressive, and so is the sense of recession and the balance of the houses on the left with the domes and chimneys on the right. It has telling details such as the spectators on the balcony and the officer crossing the water towards the royal barges, but they are subordinated to the glittering and radiant impression of the whole.

Constable's large Academy picture for 1823 was "Salisbury Cathedral from the Bishop's Grounds", of which he wrote: "It was the most difficult subject in landscape I ever had upon my easel. I have not flinched at the work of the windows, buttresses (etc., etc.,), but I have as usual made my escape in the evanescence of the chiaroscuro." He seems to have used this word as a private shorthand term denoting various things — perhaps emotional expression of the phenomena of light and atmosphere "dews, breezes, bloom and freshness, not one of which has yet been perfected on the canvas of any painter in the world". "Salisbury Cathedral" illustrates how the mature Constable could preserve the spontaneity and dynamism of his oil sketches in the finished exhibition pictures; the palette knife has been freely used, dabs and flecks of pure colour show the changing movements of light, and forms are often summarised rather than depicted in detail. At the same time the full-size sketches were carried to a greater degree of finish. The Bishop of Salisbury had commissioned this picture of his cathedral; and he later ordered further copies, one of which, now in the Frick Collection, New York, is signed and dated 1826.

Ruskin wrote of Constable's "unteachableness" and lack of reverence for tradition, but such a view is strongly contradicted by his behaviour on visiting Sir George Beaumont at Cole Orton Hall about this time. Although he had now reached considerable maturity in his work and was about forty-seven years old, he was overwhelmed by the Old Masters in Beaumont's collection; he made a sketch of a Rubens' landscape but felt that the Claudes demanded more careful copies, and to make these he stayed there long after he had intended to be in London working on his large canvas for exhibition. In spite of his devotion to the old masters, he condemned the new proposals for the founding of a national Collection. "Should there be a National Gallery (which is talked of)," he wrote to Fisher, "there will be an end of the art in poor old England, and she will become, in all that relates to painting, as much a nonentity as every other country that has one. The reason is plain: the manufacturers of pictures are then made the criterion of perfection instead of nature." Constable did not fear the copying of pictures so much as the weak imitation of a style, rightly judging that not all painters could combine his veneration for tradition with individual investigation of his beloved "nature".

This, after all, was the central originality of Constable's art — that his style rested directly on visual experience rather than on idealisation and picturesque clichés. His attitude emerges clearly in his fiery disapprovals. Thus in 1820 Matthews in *The Diary of an Invalid,* writing of Glover, declared: "I believe the beauty of his pictures is in an inverse ratio to their fidelity; and that nature must be stripped of her green living, and dressed in the browns of the painters, or confined to her own autumnal tints in order to be transferred to canvas", which provoked from Constable the comment, "this is too bad, and one would throw the book out of the window, but that its grossness is its own cure." Lawrence Gowing has summarised very well this central aspect of Constable's work. "Constable," he writes, "felt the force of both nature and art, and his development was the discovery of the conflict and agreement between them", and after quoting the famous passage in the letter of 1802 cited above: "We feel so clearly in it the sense in which art and aesthetic perception must depend on the total inherited idea of art and also of the sense in which it cannot." One can see this dichotomy in Constable's apparently contradictory statements. At one minute he will write, "Art is a plant of the conservatory, not of the desert", and at another time, "The country makes pictures seem trumpery things". His devotion to immediacy, to the small germ of vivid original perception which sparks off a picture, reminds one, with all their differences, of Paul Cézanne and his *"petit sensation"*. As Constable wrote, "My pictures will never be popular, for they have no *handling* but I do not see *handling* in nature".

Many people believe that Constable's greatest masterpiece is the full-scale work for the Academy Exhibition of 1825, "The Leaping Horse", now at Burlington House; others have preferred the wonderful and dynamic sketches for it which may be seen reproduced on pp. 62, 63, which Andrew Forge in a broadcast called "the first instance of an art which is all personal expression". Although Constable used the traditional brown-toned canvas, he sets against this, not the customary gradual modulation, but extremes of light against extremes of dark, a white dazzling sky, sharp greens of meadow executed in rough, broken paint put on with the knife. As Forge says, the whole scene is concerned with "violent urgency" as a clash of light and dark, with dramatic towering trees and turbulent sky. It is imaginative rather than inventive in the way that Turner invents a make-believe atmosphere, and Constable may well have witnessed a scene very like this. But once again he has controlled and articulated his subject in impressions by basing it, like so many of his other compositions, on the pictorial conventions of the Roman school of Poussin and Claude, which involves the strong intersection of verticals and horizontals, between which he deploys the gradual movements backwards in space. Notice the square block of trees at the left and the nearly vertical stumps, trees and mast which divide the canvas into orderly compartments. Constable described "The Leaping Horse" to Fisher thus: "It is a Canal, and full of the Bustle incident to such a scene . . . with dogs, horses, boys and Men and Women and Children, and best of all old timber-props, Water plants, Willow stumps, sedges, old nets etc."

In 1824 Maria Constable's increasingly bad health caused Constable to take her to Brighton, which he complained to Fisher, "is the receptacle of the fashion and off-scouring of London. The magnificence of the sea . . . and its 'everlasting voice' is drowned in the din and tumult of stage coaches, gigs, *flys* etc. and the beach is only Piccadilly . . . by the seaside. Ladies dressed and undressed . . . footmen, children, nursery-maids, dogs, boys, fishermen; rotten fish and these hideous amphibious animals, the old bathing women . . . all mixed together in endless and indecent confusion. The genteeler part, Marine Parade, is still more unnatural with its trimmed and neat appearance, and the dandy jetty or Chain Pier, with its long elegant strides into the sea a full quarter of a mile". But Constable seemed able in later life to strike roots in other places than his beloved Suffolk, and his picture of the "Marine Parade and Chain Pier" (in the Tate Gallery), painted three years later, is at the same time an extraordinarily faithful rendering of the effects of light and atmosphere in Sussex and an epitome of his own internal drama and disquiet. He had cause for anxiety in the illness of his wife, who died in 1829, but even before this sorrow Constable's style of painting had become less serene than it had been in his mid-career. He used the palette knife increasingly and contrived to give the effect of texture in water, fields and sky. His contemporaries, for the most part, disliked his glazed highlights and called them "Constable's snow".

After his wife's death Constable was subject to fits of depression and he was often considered cantankerous and argumentative by his friends. "How for some wise purpose is every bit of sunshine clouded over in me", he wrote. "Can it be wondered at that I paint continual storms—'Tempest o'er tempest rolled'? Still the darkness is majestic and I have not to accuse myself of ever having prostituted the moral feeling of Art . . . . My canvas soothes me into a forgetfulness of the scene of turmoil and folly and worse." Other griefs followed in 1832 when he lost both the faithful John Fisher and Dunthorne's son, who had become his assistant. "Hadleigh Castle" (p. 69) particularly, perhaps, the full-scale sketch—was his elegy for Maria, and a melancholy if impressive dirge it is.

Constable's later pictures continue to show an alternation between those which are studied and finished in detail, such as "The Cornfield" (1826) (detail, p. 66), and those in which he seeks to represent his changing impressions of air, sparkling rain and dews, showing an almost total disregard of conventional technique. The latter include the stormy "Stoke by Nayland" (about 1830; p. 65) and some of his later pencil sketches of the hilly, broken downlands of Sussex (pp. 50, 51) which he visited after he had formed a new friendship (in 1834) with a namesake called George Constable who lived at Arundel. On the day that he died in 1837 he was working on his large, somewhat over-elaborated picture of this place, "Arundel Mill and Castle" (now in the Toledo Museum of Art, Ohio) constructed from these pencil sketches.

He had been elected to the Royal Academy in 1829 but he was, he wrote, "smarting under his election", since Lawrence had tactlessly told him that he was lucky to be chosen. It was also rather a sad irony that just before her death Mrs. Constable had inherited £20,000, which freed Constable from money worries but unfortunately at a time when he could no longer enjoy this fortune with her. Among other notable products of his later years are "A Dell, Helmingham" (about 1830), now in the National Gallery, which has been described as the first *sous-bois* of nineteenth-century art, and the "Stonehenge" (1836-37) (p. 49), of which Lawrence Gowing writes that in such visions of "ancient weathered grandeur his subject was not freshness but endurance". Like so many of his later works, this water colour was based on a drawing made much earlier, in 1820 (p. 48).

From about 1829 Constable, like Turner, planned to gain from his work the wider reputation of engraving, and from 1830 he began to issue a series of mezzotints under the title "English Landscape Scenery", projected to some extent as a rival of Turner's *"Liber Studiorum"* and chosen especially to arrest the more abrupt and transient appearance of the chiaroscuro of nature. Fisher had been against the scheme: "There is in your pictures too much evanescent effect and general tone to be expressed in black and white. Your charm is colour and the cool tint of English daylight. The burr of mezzotint will never touch that." It is true that Constable was more a colourist than a draughtsman and that in the mezzotints the strong contrasts of light and shade are too violent. Besides this, whereas Turner's engraver was a man of established reputation, Constable chose a young man, David Lucas, who had only just finished his apprenticeship. In spite of financial loss, under Constable's close supervision Lucas was often successful in translating the essence of the originals into black and white, notably in such radiant pastorals as "A Summerland" and "Spring, East Bergholt Common" (p. 27).

All this time Constable's art had been attracting, comparatively speaking, more attention in France than in his native country, though he himself was decidedly insular and never left England. French curiosity and appetite for English art had been whetted by the austere control exercised by David throughout the revolutionary period, so that the homely subjects of David Wilkie and landscapes without classical themes, for example, took on the savour of forbidden fruit. There was the additional factor that the art of Constable's mid-career owed a good deal to Rubens, who was in high favour in Paris at the time.

It is well known that when "The Hay Wain" (p. 33) appeared at the Salon it was highly praised by Charles Nodier, who compared it with the art of the great Dutch masters, and his account was soon published in *Promenade de Dieppe aux Montagnes d'ecosse*. Géricault too, when he came to England to exhibit the "Raft of the Medusa", returned to France almost stupefied *("tout étourdi")* by the sight of the same picture. In the next year a Parisian art dealer, John Arrowsmith, came and made Constable an offer for "The Hay Wain", then showing at the Bristol Institution. This offer was not large enough to be acceptable, but later he returned and bought the picture with the "Bridge on the River Stour" (exhibited in 1822) thrown in. Subsequently he ordered six more pictures and in 1823 another work of Constable's went to the Continent—a sketch belonging to Jacques Auguste Regnier, a painter of historical landscapes and an admirer of Walter Scott. Delacroix went round to see it and described it in his journal as *"admirable chose et exquise"*. Frederic Villot, who taught Delacroix etching, has left an account of its well-known effect on "The Massacre of Scio". Delacroix was apparently struck by the brilliance and texture of "The Hay Wain" and returning to his studio where "The Massacre" was almost finished, he introduced rich semitones, gave transparency to the trees by means of glazing and added impasto (thick pigment) for the lights. Villot adds that Delacroix had at once surprised one of Constable's secrets—"the subdivision of colours".

In 1824 Arrowsmith returned to London accompanied by another French dealer, Claude Schroth, who ordered three pictures, two of which he wished to be Hampstead views. Something of the sensation caused in Paris by the arrival of the Constables can be estimated by the alarm of the orthodox critics, one of whom begged artists not te be seduced from their loyalty to Poussin by works so sketchy and lacking in form. But the young rebels, the Romantics, looked upon the English as their allies, and Adolphe Thiers wrote that Constable's art displayed "delicacy, perspective and truth"; and, to use the usual expression, "it is full of air". Stendhal criticised the negligence of Constable's brushwork and his lack of *"idéal"* but declared that "The Hay Wain" completely eclipsed the French landscapes hanging near it. "I have given my enthusiastic praise to Mr. Constable. That is because truth for me has an irresistible appeal." The artist William Brockedon, who was passing through Paris at the time, sent a note telling Constable that he had created a sensation in the French school of landscape. "The next exhibition in Paris will teem with your imitators, or the school of nature versus the school of Birmingham."

When Delacroix came to England in 1825, he was furnished with a letter to Constable, and it was probably from conversation at this time that he was later able to record in his journal: "Constable says that the superiority of the greens in his meadows is due to the fact that they are made up of a large number of different greens. What gives a lack of intensity and life to the verdure of the ordinary run of landscape painters is that they do it with a uniform tint." Other French visitors to Constable about this time included Didot and Henri Monnier; one of his visitors asked him what his method was, to which Constable replied that he had none. In the same year "The White Horse" was sent to Lille, where it was awarded a second gold medal. Later on, when he sent "The Cornfield" to the Salon of 1827, the novelty had paled and his work was not much discussed.

But the point had been taken, and Paul Huet, in his notes for a history of French landscape, speaks of the magnificent lesson which Constable had given them in 1824. It was apparently more Constable's technique than his subject matter which threw many French artists into *"un trouble profond"*. Délécluze, who was far from favourable to Constable, admitted that his pictures in the Salon of 1824 had made the French realise "how heavy, insensitive and false was their colouring ... he was imitated and is still being imitated". Early examples of this influence are Huet's "Distant View of Rouen" (c. 1828) and landscapes by Camille Flers. Delacroix, who presided over the meetings of the landscape painters who were seeking to have the work of Rousseau admitted to the Salon, spoke of Constable as "the father of our School of landscape", and Thackeray, who had known Paris as an art student, took the same view. The chief novelties which they found in his work were the use of vivid colours divided into component elements, homely scenery without classical themes and an interest in the sky as a source of light—an interest later to be carried much further by the impressionists. The Barbizon painters, who began to group themselves together as a school about 1830, differed in their approach to painting and the extent to which they were influenced by Constable. Theodore Rousseau saw "The Hay Wain" in 1833, and it made a great impression on him, especially as he shared Constable's passion for trees, of which Leslie writes: "I have seen him admire a fine tree with an ecstasy of delight like that with which he would catch up a beautiful child in his arms." Dupré was also indebted to Constable, whose work he probably saw on a visit to England, particularly in some English sea-scapes such as *"Vue prise à Southampton"*, exhibited in 1835. Troyon's broken forms and colours probably derive from Constable, and more than all the others Daubigny's sunsets painted in bold, free brushstrokes recall the "chiaroscuro" of nature depicted in Constable's oil sketches. None of them painted "the light that never was on sea or land". Later on, the Impressionists, in their interest in the transitory and in light, proved themselves to be Constable's heirs, and Monet might have echoed his "I never saw an ugly thing in my life, for let the form of an object be what it will—light, shade and perspective will make it beautiful".

Such records as we have of Constable's various lectures afford further insight into his views on landscape painting. One of his favourite examples was Titian's "Peter Martyr", which he considered "the foundation of all the styles of landscape in every school of Europe in the following century"; other works to which he often alluded and to which he accorded high praise were Poussin's "Deluge", "The Rainbow" by Rubens and "The Mill" by Rembrandt, of whom he said, "Chiaroscuro is the great feature that characterises his art and was carried further by him than by any other painter, not excepting Corregio". Poussin was praised for seeing that "by simplicity of treatment, the most awful subjects may be made far more affecting than by over-loading them with imagery". Chiaroscuro was defined as "that power which creates space", and Constable often in his lectures struck upon some profound if simple truth such as his saying, "We see nothing truly until we understand it".

Constable's reputation never, perhaps, sank so low as Leslie complained, witness the steady trade in forgeries of his work since the 1850's. His fame in England increased greatly after 1888, when Miss Isabel Constable gave numerous oil sketches to the Victoria and Albert Museum; hitherto there had been small opportunity for seeing these, perhaps the most original and striking examples of his art. The Georgian movement in English poetry with its insistence on the less dramatic, more homely aspect of the English countryside, also coincided with — or, more probably, furthered — a growth in the appreciation of his works.

One can perhaps exaggerate the debt owed to Constable by the Barbizon painters, and through them by the Impressionists, though nowadays, since the criticisms of Douglas Cooper, it is perhaps more usual to underrate his influence. But even if this is set aside, Constable's pictures are delightful and significant in their own right; as we have seen, they well embody that solemn, almost moralistic attitude to nature which characterised the heroic early phase of the Romantic movement. Later on, the destructive side of nature loomed larger, and there emerged, on one hand, that fascination with decay and cruelty which Mario Praz described so fully in *The Romantic*

Agony and, on the other, the extreme literalness and sentimentality beloved by many Victorians. But Constable showed that the mind could be excited and elevated without the use of gross and violent stimuli; he had sentiment but was not usually sentimental. His pictures splendidly embody and express the feeling of his contemporary William Wordsworth:

> Paradise and groves,
> Elysian, Fortunate Fields—why should they be
> A history only of departed things,
> Or a mere fiction of what never was?
> For the discerning intellect of Man,
> When wedded to this goodly universe
> In love and holy passion, shall find these
> A simple produce of the common day.

LIST OF ILLUSTRATIONS

(Note: V.A.M. – Victoria & Albert Museum, London, England)

Page

48 STONEHENGE
1820; pencil; $4\frac{1}{2}\times7\frac{3}{8}$ in.; V.A.M.

49 STONEHENGE
1836-37; pencil and water colour; 6×10 in.; V.A.M.

50 ARUNDEL MILL AND CASTLE
1835; pencil; $8\frac{5}{8}\times11$ in.; V.A.M.

51 FITTLEWORTH MILL AND BRIDGE ON THE ROTHER, SUSSEX
1834; pencil; $8\frac{1}{8}\times10\frac{3}{4}$ in.; V.A.M.

52 TREES AND A SKETCH OF WATER ON THE STOUR
1830-36; pencil and sepia wash; $8\times6\frac{3}{8}$ in.; V.A.M.

53 A SLUICE, PERHAPS ON THE STOUR
1830-36; oil on paper laid on canvas; $8\frac{5}{8}\times7\frac{3}{8}$ in.; V.A.M.

54 THE THAMES, WITH WATERLOO BRIDGE
About 1819; pen, bistre and India ink; $6\frac{1}{2}\times10\frac{3}{4}$ in.; V.A.M.

55 WATERLOO BRIDGE FROM WHITEHALL STREET STAIRS
About 1819; oil on millboard; $11\frac{1}{2}\times19$ in.; V.A.M.

56 BRIGHTON BEACH, WITH FISHING BOATS AND THE CHAIN PIER
About 1824; pen, pencil and water colour;
$7\times10\frac{1}{4}$ in.; V.A.M.

57 BRIGHTON BEACH, WITH COLLIERS
1824; oil on paper; $5\frac{3}{4}\times9\frac{3}{4}$ in.; V.A.M.

58 BEACH SCENE, WITH BOATS AND FISHERMEN
About 1824; pen, pencil and grey ink; $7\times10\frac{1}{8}$ in.; V.A.M.

59 BRIGHTON BEACH
1824; oil on paper; $6\frac{1}{2}\times12$ in.; V.A.M.

60 STUDY OF TREE TRUNKS
About 1821; oil on paper; $9\frac{3}{4}\times11\frac{1}{2}$ in.; V.A.M.

61 STUDY OF SKY AND TREES WITH RED HOUSE, HAMPSTEAD
1821; oil on paper; $9\frac{1}{2}\times11\frac{3}{4}$ in.; V.A.M.

62 SKETCH FOR "THE LEAPING HORSE"
About 1824; ink and chalk; 8×11 in.;
British Museum, London

63 OIL STUDY FOR "THE LEAPING HORSE"
   About 1825; oil on canvas; 51×74 in.; V.A.M.

64 MEN LOADING A BARGE ON THE STOUR
   1827; pencil, pen and grey wash; 8⅞×13 in.; V.A.M.

65 STOKE BY NAYLAND, SUFFOLK
   About 1830; oil on paper; 9¾×13 in.; V.A.M.

66 THE CORNFIELD (detail)
   1826; oil on canvas; 56¼×48 in.; National Gallery, London

67 STUDY FOR "THE VALLEY FARM"
   About 1835; oil on canvas; 10×8¼ in.; V.A.M.

68 OLD SARUM
   1829; oil on thin card; 5⅝×8¼ in.; V.A.M.

69 HADLEIGH CASTLE
   1829; oil on canvas; 48¼×66 in.; Tate Gallery, London

70 SALISBURY CATHEDRAL FROM THE SOUTHWEST
   1811; black and white chalk; 7⅝×11¾ in.; V.A.M.

71 SALISBURY CATHEDRAL FROM THE RIVER
   About 1827; oil on canvas; 20¾×30¼ in.;
   National Gallery, London

72 WATER MEADOWS NEAR SALISBURY
   1829; oil on canvas; 18×21¾ in.; V.A.M.